GAIN THE WHOLE WORLD?

What *really* matters in life

C.B.MARTIN

Published by 10Publishing, a division of 10ofThose Limited.

10Publishing, a division of 10ofthose.com

9D Centurion Court, Leyland, PR25 3UQ, England.

Email: info@10ofthose.com Website: www.10ofthose.com

ISBN: 9781909611757

Design and typeset by: Design Chapel / www.design-chapel.com

Printed by: CPI, London.

CONTENTS

DEDICATION

For all the helpers and leaders I've served with on
Colwyn Bay 2, Bruton 2 and Quantock 3.

Colossians 1:28,29

INTRODUCTION

What good is it for someone to gain the whole world, yet forfeit their soul?

(Mark 8:36)

Have you ever tried to catch a monkey? Apparently it's quite easy. Get yourself a glass jar with a narrow neck. Stick a nice tasty banana in the bottom and wait. Once the monkey sees the banana it will slide its hand into the jar, but the clever part is this: when the monkey grabs on to the banana, it can't get its fist out of the jar. The greedy monkey won't leave the banana, so it's trapped with a massive jar on its arm. Clinging on to a fairly mediocre banana has cost it its freedom.

We're not monkeys, but we can hold on to things just as tightly and stupidly. What gets in the way of you thinking about what's really important in life? A recent survey of teenagers rated schoolwork, Facebook and the Internet as the top three distractions that stopped them focusing on God. Let's face it, nobody is going to die wishing they had got a better grade in GCSE geography, or had written just one or two more witty status updates.

What is life really about? Where did we come from? Where are we going? Jesus Christ claims to have all the answers, but like the foolish monkey, we're too busy hanging on to things which look attractive to take Him seriously.

This book will look at the things we set our hearts on instead of Jesus. Good things, some of them; things that the world around us prizes highly. But anything you put in God's place will ultimately let you down and destroy you. The Bible calls them idols. Idols aren't just disappointing, they can be deadly. We can 'gain the world' – live for pleasure, get rich, be popular – but if we lose our souls in the process we are as stuffed as that monkey. Jesus has come to set us free from the worthless fake gods, which can dominate our lives and trap us.

Take a look at Mark chapter 8.

Jesus and his disciples went on to the villages around Caesarea Philippi. On the way he asked them, 'Who do people say I am?'

They replied, 'Some say John the Baptist; others say Elijah; and still others, one of the prophets.'

'But what about you?' he asked. 'Who do you say I am?'

Peter answered, 'You are the Messiah.'

Jesus warned them not to tell anyone about him.

He then began to teach them that the Son of Man must suffer many things and be rejected by the elders, the chief priests and the teachers of the law, and that he must be killed and after three days rise again. He spoke plainly about this, and Peter took him aside and began to rebuke him.

THE SON OF MAN MUST SUFFER MANY THINGS AND BE REJECTED.

But when Jesus turned and looked at his disciples, he rebuked Peter. 'Get behind me, Satan!' he said. 'You do not have in mind the concerns of God, but merely human concerns.'

Then he called the crowd to him along with his disciples and said: 'Whoever wants to be my disciple must deny themselves and take up their cross and follow me. For whoever wants to save their life will lose it, but whoever loses their life *for me and for the gospel will save it. What good is it for someone to gain the whole world, yet forfeit their soul? Or what can anyone give in exchange for their soul? If anyone is ashamed of me and my words in this adulterous and sinful generation, the Son of Man will be ashamed of them when he comes in his Father's glory with the holy angels.' (Mark 8:27–38)*

These verses are at the heart of Mark's Gospel and, indeed, the Christian faith. Up to this point, the disciples have been pretty slow to work out who Jesus is. But here Peter has finally begun to realise that He is more than just a prophet, a teacher or a good man. He's the Christ, the Messiah, God's King. This means He is at the centre of everything; He is indescribably significant and important. But what comes next?

HE IS MORE THAN JUST A PROPHET, A TEACHER OR A GOOD MAN.

Instead of a giant plan to overthrow the Roman oppressors and free God's people, Jesus says something altogether unexpected:

He then began to teach them that the Son of Man must suffer many things and be rejected by the elders, the chief priests and the teachers of the

law, and that he must be killed and after three
days rise again. (v. 31)

You can understand Peter being a bit stunned. It doesn't sound like much of a plan. When the Prime Minister makes a victory speech after winning the election, they usually promise to improve education, create jobs and boost morale. Jesus is promising that He, the Son of Man, will face suffering, rejection and death.

But this is the type of King Christians follow. One who gave up everything for us. When we try to replace the God who made and loves us with other things, it's like a slap in His face. God is rightly angry with us. But Jesus saved us from the consequences of God's anger when He faced it, for us, on the cross. He deserves first place in our hearts because He put us first when He died for us.

Jesus outshines and out-performs any idol. He offers us life to the max; life as God intended. But if we are going to follow Him, it will be tough. It will mean giving up a 'do things my way' attitude and saying (as Jesus later did in the garden of Gethsemane) 'not my will, Lord, but yours' (Luke 22:42). That's what Jesus means by 'Whoever wants to be my disciple must deny themselves and take up their cross and follow me' in verse 34.

That may not sound desperately appealing. It might mean denying ourselves things that we'd like to have – money, success, popularity, academic achievement, certain relationships and all that goes with them. But see what Jesus is promising – a chance to gain what matters most.

You see, Jesus isn't just talking the talk when He warns us that 'whoever wants to save their life will lose it, but whoever loses their life for me and for the gospel will save it' (v. 35). Jesus lived it first. He walked the road to execution. He gave His life for us. That's why He can offer us true security, meaning and eternal life when He comes again in 'his Father's glory with the holy angels' (v. 38).

JESUS ISN'T JUST OUR RESCUER. HE IS THE KING OF THE UNIVERSE.

Let's be clear: the flipside of all of this is that we can gain the whole world with a steely determination to succeed, to be the best, to have it all, but we will put our souls at risk in the process.

Jesus isn't just our rescuer. He is the King of the Universe. He deserves all our love, honour and loyalty. One day He will return in glory, and He warns us that if we are ashamed of Him now then He will be ashamed of us then. There's a major warning here.

As you read on, take a good hard look at some of the idols that threaten to replace Jesus as your Saviour and King. Good things, some of them, but things that have become 'gods'. Be honest with yourself – are these things getting in the way of a relationship with the true and living God who made you and loves you? Take a look at just how awesome Jesus is and start to loosen your grip on that banana.

A candle is pretty bright in the darkness, but when the sun comes up it is outclassed and outshone.

C.B. Martin

Spring 2014

CHAPTER 1:

RESCUE ME!

It's not much fun running a relationship on a set of rules. One particularly tidy flatmate of mine used to leave Post-it notes on our dirty plates, reminding us of the house rules if we forgot to do the washing-up!

But ask most people what the Bible is about and at some point you'll get someone saying that it's a bunch of rules. And yes, there are rules in the Bible. Probably the most famous of these are the Ten Commandments, and as we'll see they have a lot to say about this issue of idolatry – putting something else in God's place. But if we think they are just a set of rules then we're slightly missing the point. Check out Exodus 20:1–6:

And God spoke all these words:

'I am the LORD your God, who brought you out of

Egypt, out of the land of slavery.

'You shall have no other gods before me.

'You shall not make for yourself an image in the form of anything in heaven above or on the earth beneath or in the waters below. You shall not bow down to them or worship them; for I, the LORD your God, am a jealous God, punishing the children for the sin of the parents to the third and fourth generation of those who hate me, but showing love to a thousand generations of those who love me and keep my commandments.

RESCUE, NOT RULES

Imagine you're in a lifeboat. A whole load of you have been rescued from a sinking ship, and there are still some people in the water. You know it's going to be a few hours before you get to shore, so you decide there needs to be a few ground rules to keep you safe inside the boat: No pushing or shoving, no leaning over the side, making sure that food and water are shared equally, etc.

If you shouted to the people still in the water, 'Oi! No pushing. And make sure you share the food!' it wouldn't be much help to them. They haven't been rescued and the rules can't save them.

In the same way, if you're not a Christian, what is the point of following God's guidelines? They can't rescue you, and they won't make any sense until you've been taken aboard the lifeboat. That's why the Ten Commandments (and the rest of the Law given to Moses) don't begin with a 'thou shalt' or 'thou shalt not'. Instead they begin with what God has done. He brought them 'out of Egypt, out of the land of slavery' (Exod. 20:2). God's people have already been rescued. The rules don't save them; they show them the best way to live as God's rescued people.

So how *does* God want His people to live? Well, first, He wants to be number one in their hearts – and that's closely followed by this command not to make images or idols to worship. These two commands go together.

Human beings are natural worshippers. We were made to worship God. Psalm 86:9 tells us that 'All the nations you have made will come and worship before you, Lord; they will bring glory to your name'. If we are not worshipping God, then something else will slide into the centre of our hearts and lives to fill the vacuum.

Unfortunately, as soon as the Israelites take their eyes off God, this is exactly what happens . . .

When the people saw that Moses was so long in coming down from the mountain, they gathered round Aaron and said, 'Come, make us gods who will go before us. As for this fellow Moses who brought us up out of Egypt, we don't know what has happened to him.'

Aaron answered them, 'Take off the gold earrings that your wives, your sons and your daughters are wearing, and bring them to me.' So all the people took off their earrings and brought them to Aaron. He took what they handed him and made it into an idol cast in the shape of a calf, fashioning it with a tool. Then they said, 'These are your gods, Israel, who brought you up out of Egypt.' (Exod. 32:1–4)

When you read it in the cold light of day, it seems unbelievably ridiculous and stupid. How on earth could they have forgotten God so quickly? And what kind of idiot thinks a golden statue can do anything to save you? But it's worse than that. What they are really doing is trying to domesticate Him – trying to 'tame' God – rather than worshipping Him for who He really is. God wants all of the Israelites' love and obedience, but they want a God on their terms: 'Sorry, God. We'd rather You were a gold statue that doesn't ask any awkward questions or require much from us.' But before we start laughing at them, let's think about how we behave the same way.

IDENTIFY YOUR IDOLS

An idol doesn't have to be a literal statue or image, although you might have seen this sort if you have friends from a Hindu background, for example. No, an idol is anything or anyone who takes God's place in our hearts and lives.

It is worth saying that many of our idols are good things. Unfortunately, they have become 'god things'. We use them to do things they were never created to do. It is God who is the real King of our lives, who gives us meaning, who loves us, rules us and whose opinion of us truly matters. But idols sell us the false promise that they can do all these things.

Do you ever see those adverts on Facebook claiming that all you have to do is click 'like' and you could win an iPad, a range of make-up or a huge sum of money? They are nearly always scams, ways to get hold of your data to sell on to marketing companies or lame 'get rich quick' schemes.

Idols are not just an annoying let down but a dangerous scam – they promise so much, but when it matters they fail to deliver. Remember Jesus' words in Mark 8:36? 'What good is it for someone to gain the whole world, yet forfeit their soul?' Idols are dangerous because they can't save us and we desperately need rescuing. We'll come back to that in a minute, but before we do, how exactly do we identify our idols? Well, here are a couple of clues.

Ask yourself this question: If you could change one thing about your life right now, what would it be? What do you spend your time day-dreaming about?

Maybe it would be to have more money, or to have a particular gadget or phone. Perhaps you long for hair extensions, a nose job or a six-pack (or all three!). Maybe you long for that boy or girl you really fancy to fall in love with you. Perhaps you dream of having more friends or being more popular. Or to have finished your exams with top grades and be off on an amazing holiday with all your mates.

BEWARE! GOOD THINGS MAKE THE BEST IDOLS.

If only . . . fill in the gap . . . life would be perfect. The problem is that if we are looking to any of these things to make us perfectly happy, then that thing or person has become an idol. None of these things might be bad in themselves, but beware! Good things make the best idols.

Or why not put it another way? What would utterly destroy you if you lost it? Your looks? Your ability to get the top marks? Sporting ability? Your boyfriend? Girlfriend? Your social circle? If it defines who you are, you'd be lost without it, or it is central to your identity, then that thing or person is an idol. Only God is able to define us, give us identity and rescue us.

SAYING 'DON'T MAKE SOMETHING INTO AN IDOL' IS EASIER SAID THAN DONE.

Have you identified your idols? So what now? Saying 'don't make something into an idol' is easier said than done. How can we avoid it?

THE ANTIDOTE TO IDOLS

We're all familiar with the idea of an antidote – if you're bitten by a deadly snake, you need medicine to counteract the poison. Or if you're Doctor Who and River Song has kissed you with poisoned lipstick then you're going to have to pull some clever regeneration-type moves. Poison needs a remedy.

Look back to the first part of Exodus 20 again. God doesn't just tell His people not to make idols, He also gives them the remedy – the antidote to idols:

I am the Lord your God, who brought you out of

Egypt, out of the land of slavery. (my emphasis)

First of all, the Lord is the only God. Idols are the Diet Coke of religion – tastes good, but with zero nutritional value. Nowhere near as satisfying as the real thing. But sadly, our world runs on virtual reality. Do you remember the episode where the usually sensible Penny in *The Big Bang Theory* gets sucked into an online game? It's only when the virtual version of Howard invites her for a drink and she's about to accept that she realises she needs help!

Come on, we're not that geeky, though, are we? Er, but hang on a minute – have you ever sat in the same room as someone and texted them instead of speaking to them? How many of your relationships are largely conducted online?

The good news is that we don't need to settle for a virtual reality; we don't need to worship some 'thing' or person. God has provided His perfect image to worship: Jesus.

The Son is the image of the invisible God
(Col. 1:15).

No one has ever seen God, but the one and only Son, who is himself God and is in closest relationship with the Father, has made him known. (John 1:18)

Take a long hard look at Jesus. Then look at the things you depend on instead of Him. They just don't compare. Jesus is the Word made flesh – God and human. He is totally powerful, completely loving, utterly dependable, and He gave His life for you. This is the second part of the remedy: **The Lord is the only one who can rescue us**.

RESCUE US FROM WHAT?

Think for a minute about the best present you ever received. It may have been wonderful, expensive, gorgeous, cute or exciting, but if you were drowning and someone threw it to you instead of a lifebelt, you'd probably be sunk. Quite literally. In the same way, our iPhones, best mates or family cannot solve all our problems. However good we look, however many 'A' grades we get, however fantastic the people around us are, they cannot do anything at all about our biggest need.

The Israelites were trapped as slaves in Egypt (Exod. 1). They needed a miraculous, powerful rescue. We are born slaves to sin and separated from God because of it. This is the big issue. 'Sin' seems an old-fashioned word, but it means anything we say and do to offend God and other people. We all get it wrong, don't we? However hard we try, we cannot meet God's perfect standards – and to be honest, most of the time we don't even *want* to try. We live in opposition to the God who made us, and we are heading for death and judgement (see Heb. 9:27).

WHEN JESUS DIED ON THE CROSS, HE 'REDEEMED' US.

But the same Lord who brought the Israelites out of Egypt, 'has rescued us from the dominion of darkness and brought us into the kingdom of the Son he loves' (Col. 1:13). When Jesus died on the cross, He 'redeemed' us. That is, He paid the price to free us from slavery to sin – living in a way that doesn't please God, and which leads to death.

Jesus' rescue is *priceless*:

> *For you know that it was not with perishable things such as silver or gold that you were redeemed from the empty way of life handed down to you from your ancestors, but with the precious blood of Christ, a lamb without blemish or defect. (1 Pet. 1:18,19)*

If you are a Christian, you know that truth, but we don't really live in it, do we? When we're faced with trouble, is prayer our first priority or a last resort? What do we rely on to help us? Our friends? Our mum or dad? Our own ability to sort things out, think quickly, or persuade others to do what we want?

Remember God's remedy: 'I am the LORD your God, **who brought you out of Egypt, out of the land of slavery'** (my emphasis).

That rescue from slavery is amazing – as a Christian, you have been freed from the consequences of your sin, and eternal death; rescued for eternal life and friendship with your creator.

IS PRAYER OUR FIRST PRIORITY OR A LAST RESORT?

When we see the real thing clearly, we won't want the fake. That's why it's so important to keep reminding ourselves how much better Jesus is than anything else we are tempted to look to for our sense of worth, purpose or security.

When it really matters, the only one worth hanging on to is Jesus. Idols cannot rescue us, or forgive us.

THINK IT OVER

- What is your biggest idol? Think back to the thing you long for, or would hate to lose. What does it promise?

- How are you tempted to rely on your idol to rescue or help you in life?

- What is it about Jesus you love most? How is what He offers better?

- Which Bible verses about Jesus would help you to remember how much better He is? Can you learn any of them? Write them on Post-it notes and stick them on your noticeboard or bathroom mirror.

CHAPTER 2:

PUTTING THE 'I' IN IDOL

Romeo and Juliet. Do they *really* love each other? Or are they just in it for themselves? Perhaps you have had to sit through English lessons about these so-called 'star-crossed lovers', but look at the evidence: When Romeo thinks Juliet is dead, he kills himself. Why? He's not sacrificing himself *for* her, but dying because he can't have her. Ditto for Juliet.

This relationship, like a lot of our relationships, is selfish – it's all about me. When you see the real thing – such as husbands giving up their places on the lifeboats of the *Titanic* for their wives – you know that true love is not selfish, but self-sacrificial.

This 'Romeo and Juliet' attitude is at the heart of our next idol, and indeed the book of Judges.

After the excitement of God's people being rescued from Egypt and the thrill of entering the Promised Land, things start to go badly wrong. The book of Judges is a major low point in the history of God's people. It basically goes like this:

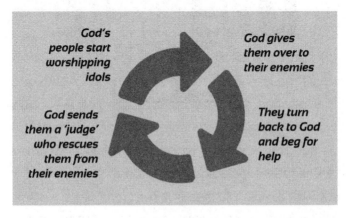

God's people start worshipping idols

God gives them over to their enemies

God sends them a 'judge' who rescues them from their enemies

They turn back to God and beg for help

We're back to the problem of idolatry again, and in a big way. As soon as God's people take their eyes off Him, they start filling the void with all sorts of idols – mostly the false gods of the countries around them, usually random fertility gods such as Baal and Asherah. This might seem a million miles away from our culture, but think what these idols offered – including abundant food and lots of sex.

But the bottom line to all this idolatry is more complicated than it seems – their real idols were not

Baal and Asherah. No, the real idol gets pointed out as the writer of Judges repeats this line:

In those days Israel had no king; everyone did as they saw fit. (Judg. 17:6; 21:25)

THE REAL IDOL IS ME

Did you spot the real idol? It's ourselves. Our desire to do whatever we like, to be the boss, to be our own god. This, if you like, is the heart of our sin – it takes us all the way back to Genesis 3, when Adam and Eve decided that they weren't going to live God's way but make their own rules. An epic fail which has plagued the world ever since. Every single one of their descendents, including you and me, has followed in their footsteps. 'Me first, God last.'

The problem is that just as the earth was designed to orbit around the sun, we were created to find the centre of our lives in God. You take the earth out of orbit, and disaster! Let's not fool ourselves about the consequences of a 'me-centred' life; they are pretty disastrous, too.

There are lots of ways in which this idol of self shows itself. Most of our actions and attitudes can be traced back to a selfish desire for our own personal satisfaction, status or security.

Think about the decisions you have made in the last week. Were any of them purely altruistic – that is, putting another person's needs and wishes above your own, even if it meant great personal inconvenience? I'm guessing not many, if any at all.

Perhaps the most obvious way that this 'me first' attitude shows itself is when it comes to sex and relationships. Most of our relationships are selfish at heart. It's when this idol of 'me first' affects sex that things get particularly messy. We see plenty of examples of this in the book of Judges. It's there in the worship of the fertility idols with their 'religious' excuses for casual sex and prostitution. We also see it in the careless attitude towards sexual relationships we read about in the last few chapters of Judges.

LET'S NOT FOOL OURSELVES ABOUT THE CONSEQUENCES OF A 'ME-CENTRED' LIFE.

Grab your Bible and read Judges chapter 19. It's pretty gruesome. In one night we get adultery, unfaithfulness, attempted male rape, appalling treatment of women, actual rape and murder, followed by the dismembering of the poor victim's body. No wonder verse 30 says:

Everyone who saw it was saying to one another,
'Such a thing has never been seen or done,
not since the day the Israelites came up out of
Egypt. Just imagine! We must do something!
So speak up!'

But as verse 1 reminded us, 'In those days Israel had no king.' If there is no king – no force for good or restraining evil – then anything goes. The book of Judges pulls no punches. Israel is in a total mess by chapter 21. They desperately need a permanent, perfect King, rather than a series of judges, or lots of mini me-first 'kings' whose selfishness and evil are unrestrained, as we see later on in Israel's history. Is this really so different to the attitude we see in the world around us?

IF IT FEELS GOOD, DO IT

'Everyone else is doing it. It's OK if it makes you feel good. You have a right to express yourself however you want. As long as it's not hurting anyone else it's fine. Don't repress your natural urges.'

Notice that all these attitudes put us and our wishes, our feelings and our desires at the centre. We are to be our own moral police. We are god in our own lives. And it's a very appealing way to live isn't it? But beware! We have made our selfish desires into an idol to worship.

In our society, sex and relationships are often bigged up as the key to self-fulfilment – there is no place for singleness or self-control, even though the Bible says the first is a good gift from God (1 Cor. 7:8) and the second a fruit of the Holy Spirit (Gal. 5:23).

It's all about self-fulfilment, self-actualization and self-satisfaction with no self-control. But what good is it for someone to sleep with 1,000 people or party at the Playboy mansion if in doing so they forfeit their soul?

Have you ever heard the cheesy line 'There's no "I" in "TEAM"'? Naff but true. If you hog the ball the whole time in a football match, you're not going to be very popular with your team mates and you're unlikely to win the match either. Football is a team game. And sex, as designed by God, is not a solo sport, either.

Check out what 1 Corinthians 7:3–5 says about the purpose of sex.

The husband should fulfil his marital duty to his wife, and likewise the wife to her husband. The wife does not have authority over her own body but yields it to her husband. In the same way, the husband does not have authority over his own body but yields it to his wife. Do not deprive each other except perhaps by mutual consent and for a time, so that you may devote yourselves to prayer. Then come together again so that Satan will not tempt you because of your lack of self-control.

Sex was designed to be a wonderful and fun way of sharing love within marriage. It works best when each person thinks about how to make their spouse happy. It's not individualistic but other-person centred.

Did you see the YouTube clip of Tom Fletcher from McFly's wedding? He basically sings his way through all his speeches, ending with a song for his new wife called 'It's All About You, Baby', and that's what true love (and sex!) should be like.

IT'S NO LONGER ALL ABOUT ME, BUT ABOUT US.

When Jesus refers to the creation of marriage in Genesis 2:24, saying, 'a man will leave his father and mother and be united to his wife, and the two will become one flesh' (Matt. 19:5), it is all about the end of selfishness. It's no longer all about *me*, but about *us*.

But, mind-blowingly, God's purpose for sex and

marriage is even more than that. Grab your Bible and read Ephesians 5:25–32. Marriage and sex is a picture of Jesus and His church – the true Bride and Bridegroom. It's important we get it right, because when we do it gives us a little glimpse of the heavenly marriage we are headed for, one built on true love and self-sacrifice. Like the men giving up their places on the *Titanic*'s lifeboats for their wives, Jesus puts His Bride – us – first, laying down His life to make us acceptable to His Father, God.

But the idol of self-interest, self-fulfilment and self-pleasing is very powerful in our world, so this is not how we are taught to think about sex and relationships. Just stop for a minute and see if you can work out the problem with these scenarios:

- Looking at online porn.
- Passing on a sexting pic of a girl from school sent by one of your mates.
- Obsessing about being single, and desperate to be in a relationship.
- Masturbating over a fantasy in your head or a picture on the Internet.
- Being pressured to go further than you want sexually by a boyfriend or girlfriend.
- Getting off with someone at a party (or going even further) knowing you won't see them again.

Are any of these things even close to the original design for sex? But they all please the idol of self.

KILLING THE IDOL OF SELFISHNESS

This idol is a tough one to kill because it wraps itself tightly around us. Wrong use of sex is just one symptom of the 'illness' of idolatry, but it's a serious one. The Bible writers talk about dealing with this idol in the starkest terms:

> Put to death, therefore, whatever belongs to your earthly nature: sexual immorality, impurity, lust, evil desires and greed, which is idolatry. (Col. 3:5)

The apostle Paul recognised that all the things above – sexual immorality, lust, greed – are idolatry, the idol being our 'earthly nature', that is, our self-centred, sinful self.

Don't think that the Bible is suggesting you have to get rid of your actual self here. Self-centredness and selfishness are like a parasite. Have you ever had warts or a verucca? One treatment to get rid of them is to blast them off with liquid nitrogen – it stings like crazy as your foot or fingers warm up again, but it kills the virus.

There is something even more effective than liquid nitrogen for killing the virus of self-centredness. In the verses just before this, Paul reminds Christians that this old way of living, the idol of selfishness, has been dealt with – it was killed on the cross with Jesus. We are now living new lives, raised from the dead with Christ, and living with Him at the centre. Paul tells these new Christians to *be* what they already *are* in Christ.

Therefore, as God's chosen people, holy and dearly loved, clothe yourselves with compassion, kindness, humility, gentleness and patience. Bear with each other and forgive one another if any of you has a grievance against someone. Forgive as the Lord forgave you. And over all these virtues put on love, which binds them all together in perfect unity. Let the peace of Christ rule in your hearts, since as members of one body you were called to peace. And be thankful. Let the message of Christ dwell among you richly as you teach and admonish one another with all wisdom through psalms, hymns, and songs from the Spirit, singing to God with gratitude in your hearts. And whatever you do, whether in word or deed, do it all in the name of the Lord Jesus, giving thanks to God the Father through him.
(Col. 3:12–17)

Holy! The parasites scraped off, the viruses blasted away. This is who you were created to be; your true self in Christ. Imagine being like this all the time – no stupid arguments with people, no broken friendships, messy break-ups and epic rows at home. This is who we *truly* are, if we are trusting in Jesus.

As soon as you get a place at uni you *are* a student, but it takes a while to get your student ID, to work out how to use the library and how to boil a Pot Noodle. You have to learn how to *be* a student. So how do we learn to be what we already are in Christ? Look at these other-people centred words in the passage above– we are to clothe ourselves with 'compassion, kindness, humility, gentleness and patience'. You can't practise any of these virtues in a vacuum; they are all defined by how we treat other people. This applies whether you are in a relationship or not – we are all called to live in community. Paul also stresses forgiveness and love. Why do we need those? Because they are how Christ treated us, and He is the one who enables us to treat others that way.

THIS IS WHO YOU WERE CREATED TO BE; YOUR TRUE SELF IN CHRIST.

So when the idol of self is clamouring for your attention, look at Jesus. Then look at other people. Jesus gave up everything for you. He loves you, He forgives you. Ask for His help to put other people first – act in their best interests, not just for what you can get out of them. They are precious to God because Jesus died for them, so treat them with respect.

The remedy for the idol of self?

> Jesus replied: "'Love the Lord your God with all your heart and with all your soul and with all your mind." This is the first and greatest commandment. And the second is like it: "Love your neighbour as yourself."' (Matt. 22:37–39)

It's not 'me first' but God first. It's not everyone doing 'as they saw fit' but looking first to the interests of others just like Jesus did (Phil. 2:4–8):

> not looking to your own interests but each of you to the interests of the others.
>
> In your relationships with one another, have the same mindset as Christ Jesus:
>
> Who, being in very nature God,
>
> did not consider equality with God something to be used to his own advantage;
>
> rather, he made himself nothing
>
> by taking the very nature of a servant,

being made in human likeness.
And being found in appearance as a man,
he humbled himself
by becoming obedient to death –
even death on a cross!

We can't do this in our own strength. No, *we* certainly can't, but Jesus always lived this way and as Colossians 3:3 reminds us, 'you died, and your life is now hidden with Christ in God'. So be what you are.

THINK IT OVER

- In what areas of your life are you most selfish?
- How are you tempted to please the idol of selfishness in the area of sex and relationships?
- What is so good about the way God designed sex?
- How can you 'put to death' your idol of self?

CHAPTER 3:

THE MEANING OF LIFE?

In Lily Allen's song 'The Fear' she sings in the persona of a fame-hungry wannabe on a mission to be thin, fabulous, famous and rich (if fake!). Yet the chorus reminds us that despite seeming to have it all, she is full of fear and confusion as she desperately searches for meaning.

The guy in the Bible passage we're about to look at also had it all, but he was determined to work out what the purpose of life was.

After the anarchy we saw in the book of Judges comes the relative peace and prosperity of life under King David and King Solomon. Israel had a God-ordained ruler and things seemed pretty sorted. But even with the blatant idolatry and disobedience wiped out, people still faced the temptation to put other things in God's place.

THE QUEST FOR MEANING

The book of Ecclesiastes has a very modern feel to it. It was probably written by King Solomon who narrates the book as the character 'the Teacher'. His refrain at the beginning 'Meaningless! Meaningless! . . . Everything is meaningless'[1] sets the tone for the whole book. In the opening chapters, the Teacher sets out to experiment with various ways of living in his search for fulfilment, meaning and purpose. If he was, indeed, Solomon, then he had the known world at his feet.

The three approaches he focuses on in chapter 2 are possessions, pleasure and wisdom. In our world we might call them the idols of stuff, fun and academic success.

Let's see what he's got to say:

> I said to myself, 'Come now, I will test you with pleasure to find out what is good.' But that also proved to be meaningless. 'Laughter,' I said, 'is

*madness. And what does pleasure accomplish?'
I tried cheering myself with wine, and embracing
folly – my mind still guiding me with wisdom. I
wanted to see what was good for people to do
under the heavens during the few days of their
lives.*

*I undertook great projects: I built houses for myself
and planted vineyards. I made gardens and parks
and planted all kinds of fruit trees in them. I made
reservoirs to water groves of flourishing trees. I
bought male and female slaves and had other
slaves who were born in my house. I also owned
more herds and flocks than anyone in Jerusalem
before me. I amassed silver and gold for myself,
and the treasure of kings and provinces. I acquired
male and female singers, and a harem as well –
the delights of a man's heart. I became greater by
far than anyone in Jerusalem before me. In all this
my wisdom stayed with me.*

*I denied myself nothing my eyes desired;
    I refused my heart no pleasure.
My heart took delight in all my labour,
    and this was the reward for all my toil.
Yet when I surveyed all that my hands had done
    and what I had toiled to achieve,*

everything was meaningless, a chasing after the wind;

    nothing was gained under the sun.

Then I turned my thoughts to consider wisdom,

    and also madness and folly.

What more can the king's successor do

    than what has already been done?

I saw that wisdom is better than folly,

    just as light is better than darkness.

The wise have eyes in their heads,

    while the fool walks in the darkness;

but I came to realise

    that the same fate overtakes them both.

Then I said to myself,

'The fate of the fool will overtake me also.

    What then do I gain by being wise?'

I said to myself,

    'This too is meaningless.'

For the wise, like the fool, will not be long remembered;

    the days have already come when both have been forgotten.

Like the fool, the wise too must die!

STUFF

In the trailer for *Money Never Sleeps*, the sequel to the 1980s classic movie, *Wall Street*, the baddie, Gordon Gekko, is let out of prison. We see him collecting his belongings, an expensive suit, cufflinks, gold watch etc. Then he is given his mobile phone. It's an absolute brick – highly desirable in 1987 – a total joke today.

It doesn't take long for our most prized possessions to lose their appeal. Think back to Christmas. What was your best present? A One Direction toothbrush? An Angry Birds onesie? How much did you look forward to getting it? Exactly how long was it before you took it for granted and moved on to the next must-have item? As we've seen, mobile phones are a classic example of this – the manufacturers and advertisers build dissatisfaction into even the shiniest and slickest new handset by bringing out a better version only months after the last one. The smartphone you were so proud of when you took it out of the box soon seems out of date and unimpressive.

THINK BACK TO CHRISTMAS. WHAT WAS YOUR BEST PRESENT?

The Teacher didn't have access to the electronic gadgets we love so much, but he was wealthier than any of us. Check out verses 4 to 9; an extensive property portfolio, major assets, serious bling and a whole host of servants and girlfriends. This guy had it all.

But what is his conclusion (look at verses 11, 17 and 18)? It's meaningless.

Why? Because, bluntly, you can't take it with you when you die. Death robs us of everything. Even the most longed-for car, house, private jet or whatever becomes utterly pointless the minute you or someone you love is faced with death. Stuff is a pretty poor idol because it doesn't last.

But you know that, right? What really matters is having fun with friends. Enjoying life – it is experiences that matter, not just material possessions.

EAT, DRINK AND BE MERRY

Some of the ancient Greek philosophers became famous for the phrase, 'Eat, drink and be merry, for tomorrow we die.' This approach is still around today. You might remember the atheist bus posters a few years ago: 'There's probably no God. Now stop worrying and enjoy your life'. But can we enjoy life without God? The Teacher decides to road-test this philosophy. Read verses 1 to 10.

He certainly appears to be embracing the party lifestyle! He got seriously wasted (v. 3), had a laugh with his mates (v. 3) and denied himself nothing; whatever he wanted he took, and whatever fun was to be had, he was part of it. (v. 10).

His conclusion? Pleasure is also meaningless. He calls it 'a chasing after wind'. Can you ever catch the wind? Nope. And pleasure, or the pursuit of pleasure, is an endless chase – it's an unstable, unreliable idol. Yes, you might have a blinding night out, but afterwards comes the hangover or the downer. So off you go in search of the next buzz, the next high. Drug addiction is the perfect example of someone who has made pleasure an idol – you become enslaved to it; you spend every waking minute searching for the next hit, the next fix, but it only lasts a short time and all the while it is slowly destroying you.

PLEASURE, OR THE PURSUIT OF PLEASURE, IS AN ENDLESS CHASE.

Even great things such as winning matches don't last. When he was just 24, Jonny Wilkinson experienced triumph in the Rugby World

Cup. It had been his ambition since he was 9 years old. How could the rest of his life be any better? As that realisation sank in, he says he began to feel the elation slipping away even during the victory lap around the stadium.

> Yet when I surveyed all that my hands had done
> > and what I had toiled to achieve,
> everything was meaningless, a chasing after the
> wind;
> > nothing was gained under the sun. (v. 11)

OK, OK, so stuff, partying or even sport doesn't provide meaning, but what about being sensible, hard-working, and academically successful? That's the purpose of life – at least, that's what your teachers and maybe even your mum or dad will tell you. Wisdom, that's where it's at.

ACADEMIC SUCCESS

The big thing that King Solomon was famous for was his wisdom. In his case, it was the wisdom to be able to rule God's people well, but with that came great learning and scholarly achievement. However, even at the beginning of the book, back in chapter 1 he tells us: 'For with much wisdom comes much sorrow; the more knowledge, the more grief' (v. 18). And as the whole book ends, he points out that 'Of making many books there is no end, and much study wearies the body' (Eccl. 12:12), something you may empathise with if you're revising for exams!

Now, wisdom, knowledge, academic success and going to the top universities are all good things, *but...* look back at what the Teacher has to say in verses 12 to 16. He's not saying wisdom is bad – it's certainly better than folly – but however much you achieve, however many GCSEs or A levels you get, you end up the same as someone with no wisdom and no education at all: 'Like the fool, the wise man too must die!'

If being clever is the source of your identity, what gives you value or makes you happy, then it's an idol, and an idol which will let you down. As soon as you fail an exam or a job interview, your whole identity and self-esteem comes crumbling down around you.

See what the apostle Paul has to say:

> *For the message of the cross is foolishness to those who are perishing, but to us who are being saved it is the power of God. For it is written:*
> *'I will destroy the wisdom of the wise;*
> *the intelligence of the intelligent I will frustrate.'*
> *. . . For the foolishness of God is wiser than*

human wisdom, and the weakness of God is
stronger than human strength. (1 Cor. 1:18,19,25)

Human wisdom will only get you so far. The biggest brain in the world couldn't have worked out how God was going to resolve the problem of judging sin and saving sinful people *at the same time*. The cross looks like a terrible mistake, absolute foolishness and failure, unless you know what God was doing.

The top professors and academics of our century have got nothing if they don't have Christ. Likewise, a person with no qualifications who knows and loves Jesus has got it all.

This is not to say don't try your best at school or college, or here's a good excuse to ditch your coursework or homework. But, in a survey I recently conducted with a group of 14- to 18-year-olds, the thing that was most likely to drag them away from spending time with God was schoolwork. Be wary about making academic success your idol.

FOR TOMORROW WE DIE

Whether your motto is 'spend, spend, spend', 'revise, revise, revise' or 'Eat, drink and be merry, for tomorrow we die', the point is that tomorrow (or one day) we will come to the end of our earthly existence. The whole book of Ecclesiastes works towards one point in chapter 12:

> *Now all has been heard;*
>> *here is the conclusion of the matter:*
> *Fear God and keep his commandments,*
>> *for this is the duty of all mankind.*
> *For God will bring every deed into judgment,*
>> *including every hidden thing,*
>> *whether it is good or evil. (vv. 13,14)*

We need to live now with God at the centre, for one day we will all die and 'God will bring every deed into judgement'. Death is not the end; it is the gateway to judgement, to meeting God face to face.

So what good is it for someone to gain the latest iPhone, a party-loving reputation or a PhD, but forfeit their soul? These things are not going to qualify you to enter into God's perfect kingdom for all eternity. Only trusting in Jesus' death and resurrection can do that.

WE NEED TO LIVE NOW WITH GOD AT THE CENTRE.

My old minister, who died from cancer, said in the months before his death that 'the end of our lives, the end of history, is a person – Jesus Christ'. He was spot on. If life is headed inevitably towards meeting the God who made you and will demand an account from you, surely the place to look for meaning is in God Himself? The Teacher's conclusion in 12:13 is 'Fear God and keep his commandments'. That's what life is about, that's the purpose, the point and the meaning.

If we're trusting in Jesus then 'fearing God' doesn't mean freaking out at the thought of facing Him on Judgement Day. We can be totally confident that we are accepted, forgiven and welcomed in Christ. But it does mean we will have a healthy respect for Him, and will want to live His way because He has given and forgiven us so much.

Knowing where we are headed makes a *huge* difference to how we live *now*. Possessions, pleasure and wisdom are good things, but they are not the answer to the meaning of life. A MENSA-level IQ is nice to have, but it won't tell you why you were born. Your friends may be great, but they cannot be with you 24/7.

YOUR FRIENDS MAY BE GREAT, BUT THEY CANNOT BE WITH YOU 24/7.

The Bible tells us who we are and *whose* we are, why we were created, why we matter and where we are headed. That's the real meaning of life, and it puts everything else into perspective.

THINK IT OVER

- Which of these – stuff, fun or academic success – do you look to for meaning?

- Why do you do that? What do these things offer or promise?

- How can you remember what life is really all about?

Note

1. The word 'meaningless' has also been translated as 'empty', 'vain', 'futile' or even 'fallen', that is, frustrated, spoiled, and far from how God wanted the world to be.

CHAPTER 4:

LOSING OUR HEARTS

Think of a soap opera or drama series you watch regularly. Chances are there's someone in it that has had, or is having, an affair with someone else – cheating on their husband or wife, or two-timing their other half. Rewind a few years and the very same couple that is now falling apart probably had a fairy tale wedding.

Remember who God is? We've seen over the last three chapters that He is the rescuing God, our King, and the One who gives our lives meaning. If you are a Christian, think back to when you first understood the gospel. These verses from 1 Peter 1 really sum it up:

Though you have not seen him, you love him; and even though you do not see him now, you believe in him and are filled with an inexpressible and glorious joy, for you are receiving the end result of your faith, the salvation of your souls. (vv. 8,9)

How could you even contemplate for a moment giving your heart to anyone else?

STEALING YOUR HEART

Fast forward to the present day and some sneaky idols are trying to steal your affection away from God. Maybe you've already given your heart to something else. That's exactly what had happened to God's people in the years since the glory days of David and Solomon.

By the prophet Ezekiel's day, God's people had given themselves over to all kinds of idolatry. Imagine the sweeping helicopter camera angle as we hit chapter 8 of the book of Ezekiel. Ezekiel gets taken on a tour of what is really going on in the Temple. Remember this was the place on earth where God met His people; it was super-holy, but look at what's going on.

MAYBE YOU'VE ALREADY GIVEN YOUR HEART TO SOMETHING ELSE.

In the sixth year, in the sixth month on the fifth

*day, while I was sitting in my house and the elders of Judah were sitting before me, the hand of the Sovereign L*ORD *came on me there. I looked, and I saw a figure like that of a man. From what appeared to be his waist down he was like fire, and from there up his appearance was as bright as glowing metal. He stretched out what looked like a hand and took me by the hair of my head. The Spirit lifted me up between earth and heaven and in visions of God he took me to Jerusalem, to the entrance of the north gate of the inner court, where the idol that provokes to jealousy stood. And there before me was the glory of the God of Israel, as in the vision I had seen in the plain.*

Then he said to me, 'Son of man, look towards the north.' So I looked, and in the entrance north of the gate of the altar I saw this idol of jealousy.

And he said to me, 'Son of man, do you see what they are doing – the utterly detestable things the Israelites are doing here, things that will drive me far from my sanctuary? But you will see things that are even more detestable.'

First, we have the idol at the north gate. Here's Ezekiel with the terrible and awesome glory of the Lord before him – a glory so immense and mighty that the first time he saw it, Ezekiel fell face down

(1:28). And yet what have God's people traded for that unimaginable glory? A measly statue which they have set up defiantly at the gate of the Temple itself. What is wrong with them?!

But it gets worse. As Ezekiel gets further inside the Temple complex, literally digging through the walls of the courtyard, he sees some pretty awful graffiti.

Then he brought me to the entrance to the court. I looked, and I saw a hole in the wall. He said to me, 'Son of man, now dig into the wall.' So I dug into the wall and saw a doorway there.

And he said to me, 'Go in and see the wicked and detestable things they are doing here.' So I went in and looked, and I saw portrayed all over the walls all kinds of crawling things and unclean animals and all the idols of Israel. In front of them stood seventy elders of Israel, and Jaazaniah son of Shaphan was standing among them. Each had a censer in his hand, and a fragrant cloud of incense was rising.

He said to me, 'Son of man, have you seen what the elders of Israel are doing in the darkness, each at the shrine of his own idol? They say, "The LORD does not see us; the LORD has forsaken the land."' Again, he said, 'You will see them doing things that are even more detestable.' (8:7–13)

We're not talking Banksy here but the sort of thing you might find inside an Egyptian pyramid. Yup, the very country that has oppressed, enslaved and murdered the Israelites is now the coolest place to look to for your religion.

And who's worshipping? Well, it's the most important guys in Israel, the leaders of the people, the seventy elders. Leading them in their idolatry, their false worship, is none other than Jazaaniah who was *supposed* to be a priest serving the Lord.

HIDING IN THE DARK

What was going on? Just like those cheating soap characters, these guys justify their cheating in verse 12 by saying, 'God doesn't see, God doesn't care.' But how wrong they are.

Isn't that the heart attitude behind all our sin? All the way back to Adam and Eve we've been hiding from God, thinking we can get away with things in the darkness. But God does see and He does care. He sees what websites we've been accessing, even if we've deleted the file history. He sees what we are reading and what we are thinking about. He sees how many hours we spend on Call of Duty or Grand

Theft Auto. He sees what's in our hearts when we play them, too.

But that's not to make us feel scared or judged – although perhaps it should. Remember, God doesn't just see; God cares. Why does God care about what we are letting into our hearts and minds?
Because He loves us.

When you were little, your mum or dad or someone else probably tried to protect you from things that would harm you or upset you. I doubt you were allowed to watch horror movies when you were 5. God is our heavenly Father and He wants to keep us safe from the things that damage us – things such as porn, violent games and movies; anything that dehumanises us or those around us.

REMEMBER, GOD DOESN'T JUST SEE; GOD CARES.

But there are other less obviously damaging idols which are also after our hearts. We've seen that the men in Ezekiel's Israel are pretty dreadful – how about the women? Just as bad.

Then he brought me to the entrance of the north gate of the house of the LORD, and I saw women sitting there, mourning the god Tammuz. He said to me, 'Do you see this, son of man? You will see

things that are even more detestable than this.'
(vv.14,15)

These ladies are mourning for Tammuz. Who was he? A Babylonian fertility god, a bit like some of the ones you read about in Greek and Roman legends, who dies to keep the crops growing. And this myth, this story, is making the girls weep. They are actually crying over someone who doesn't exist.

Random? Well, hang on a minute. Haven't we all done this? A favourite character in a book or movie dies and we get all choked up. Now, I'm not saying that crying at books or movies is wrong – I've done it myself. But we have to ask ourselves Do real things move our emotions as much? We might weep over the death of a much-loved character in a book, or swoon over Twilight's Edward or Jacob, but seriously, do we ever genuinely cry over our own sin? Or fall so deeply in love with Jesus that He is our all-consuming delight?

DO REAL THINGS MOVE OUR EMOTIONS AS MUCH?

The danger of getting obsessed with an imaginary world is that it can trick us into giving our hearts to it. We can all think of examples – fanatically following a celeb on Twitter who we will never meet, spending hours dreaming about the latest boy band pin-up, or getting sucked into Internet fanfic and endless online discussions with fellow Twihards, Trekkies, Star Wars nuts, or Cosplay obsessives.

These things aren't as obviously damaging as porn or violent images, but they can be equally seductive. We give our hearts over to them, just like the women who were emotionally obsessed with the fake god Tammuz, and we become addicted or dependent on them.

A test that is used to determine alcohol addiction is called the CAGE test:

C – cut down. *Have you ever felt the need to cut down on that thing?*

A – annoyed. *Have people annoyed you by criticizing how much time you spend on it?*

G – guilt. *Have you ever felt guilty about it?*

E – every day. *Do you ever feel you have to start the day by doing whatever it is?*

We could equally ask ourselves the same questions about whatever fantasy we have given our hearts to. We can cheat on God emotionally by becoming dependent on these make-believe heroes while being cold and distant towards the One who truly loves us.

So how does Ezekiel's journey through the Temple

end? Well, with twenty-five guys literally turning their back to God's Temple – the place where He promised to meet them and to forgive their sins – and bowing down to the sun in the east.

> He then brought me into the inner court of the house of the LORD, and there at the entrance to the temple, between the portico and the altar, were about twenty-five men. With their backs towards the temple of the LORD and their faces towards the east, they were bowing down to the sun in the east. He said to me, 'Have you seen this, son of man? Is it a trivial matter for the people of Judah to do the detestable things they are doing here? Must they also fill the land with violence and continually arouse my anger? Look at them putting the branch to their nose! Therefore I will deal with them in anger; I will not look on them with pity or spare them. Although they shout in my ears, I will not listen to them.' (8:16–18)

You might not be a sun worshipper, like these guys (even if you do like getting a tan!), but the thing to notice is that they are blatant about worshipping something other than God. It's not hidden away in the dark like the elders or getting caught up in emotion like the girls. They are what the apostle Paul calls 'glorying in their shame' (see Phil. 3:19). And we can do that too.

When we're not even ashamed or embarrassed about putting God second, it's time to worry. Being unable to remember any of the Bible, but being able to quote all the dialogue of your favourite film or TV series; spending half an hour on the phone to your boyfriend or girlfriend going 'love you, love you, you hang up first, no, you hang up first', but never bothering to talk to God in prayer; boasting on your Facebook status about missing church because 'I've got such a hangover. LOL'.

But what good is it for someone to fill their heart with trivia but forfeit their soul?

See the scary warning in verses 17 to 18. God is angry. He will not play second fiddle. He will not be cheated on. The Bible says that the church is God's beautiful, cherished Bride, and He will not just sit back and watch her give her heart to someone else. As we saw earlier, Jesus is sometimes described as the Bridegroom – He has come to woo us, to allure us, to give us His heart and to draw our hearts back to Him. Don't two-time Him. Don't let idols drag your affection away from Him.

GOD IS ANGRY. HE WILL NOT PLAY SECOND FIDDLE.

HE LOVES YOU

The book of Hosea tells the story of a prophet who is called by God to marry an unfaithful wife who, sure enough, cheats on him, betrays him and leaves him. Amazingly, God asks him to go in search of her, forgive her and take her back. Why? Because that is what He himself does for His people:

I will punish her for the days
    she burned incense to the Baals;
she decked herself with rings and jewellery,
    and went after her lovers,
    but me she forgot,'
declares the LORD.
   'Therefore I am now going to allure her;
    I will lead her into the wilderness
    and speak tenderly to her.
There I will give her back her vineyards,
    and will make the Valley of Achor a door of hope.
There she will respond as in the days of
    her youth,
    as in the day she came up out of Egypt.
(Hos. 2:13–15)

Why not go away and read Hosea's story, and think about how it echoes our behaviour towards God and His towards us?

Our sin is grim when we see it up close, and you might be feeling pretty beaten up and rubbish after thinking about it. But be encouraged that although God is rightfully angry at our unfaithfulness, He wants to forgive us; He wants to change us. Later on in Ezekiel He promises:

> *I will give them an undivided heart and put a new spirit in them; I will remove from them their heart of stone and give them a heart of flesh. Then they will follow my decrees and be careful to keep my laws. They will be my people, and I will be their God. (11:19,20)*

Only God can perform this kind of open-heart surgery. As Jesus put it when He came to earth, 'It is not the healthy who need a doctor, but the sick. I have not come to call the righteous, but sinners' (Mark 2:17).

GOD SEES AND HE CARES. HE IS REAL AND TRUE.

God sees and He cares. He is real and true. He came down from heaven to win us back, and died to show you how much He loves you. He deserves and demands all of our hearts.

THINK IT OVER

- What do you give your heart to? Try the CAGE test.
- What about it appeals to your emotions?
- Write down five ways in which Jesus is far better.

CHAPTER 5:

MONEY MONEY MONEY

When Charles Dickens came up with the character of Ebenezer Scrooge, he probably didn't realise how famous his creation would become. Everyone knows what you mean if you call someone a 'scrooge', and his distant relations can still be seen from Scrooge McDuck to Mr Burns on *The Simpsons*.

Scrooge is a classic example of someone whose idol has ended up ruling over him. And money is the idol most likely to do this to us.

Did you know that Jesus says far more about the dangers of money than He does about sexual immorality? In fact, so does the whole New Testament! But how many times have you heard it taught about, compared to the amount of time and energy spent on talking about sex? That suggests we have a pretty major blind spot when it comes to money.

THE LOVE OF MONEY

So how can money become an idol? Well, first, it's probably a good idea to point out that money itself is neutral. 1 Timothy 6:10 points out that 'the love of money is a root of all kinds of evil'. Note that it is the *love* of money that is the root of evil, not the money itself.

A pound coin isn't exactly the Darth Vader of the material world, but the uses it can be put to can be very evil indeed. You could use a pound coin to free a supermarket trolley to help an elderly person with their shopping, or use that same trolley to ram the local jewellers' window.

THE LOVE OF MONEY IS A ROOT OF ALL KINDS OF EVIL.

It's what you do with money that matters. Loving money can end up like being in an abusive relationship; if we start by loving money, it swiftly becomes our master. In Matthew 6:24 Jesus warns us that 'No one can serve two masters. Either you will hate the one and love the other, or you will be devoted to the one and despise the other. You cannot serve both God and money.'

Remember Gollum in *The Hobbit* and *The Lord of the Rings*? He is attracted to the ring, and within moments it has captivated him to the point of being willing to murder for it. Rather than him possessing it, it possesses him and gives him no peace. Tolkien writes about him always having to take it out and look at it, checking it is safe; it dominates his thoughts and every waking moment.

The idol of money has the same sort of potential to rule over us and we see that particularly clearly in the case of the rich young ruler. We meet this guy in Matthew, Mark and Luke's Gospels. Here's what is says in Matthew 19:

> Just then a man came up to Jesus and asked, 'Teacher, what good thing must I do to get eternal life?'
>
> 'Why do you ask me about what is good?' Jesus replied. 'There is only One who is good. If you want to enter life, keep the commandments.'
>
> 'Which ones?' he enquired.
>
> Jesus replied, '"You shall not murder, you shall not commit adultery, you shall not steal, you shall

not give false testimony, honour your father and mother," and "love your neighbour as yourself."'

'All these I have kept,' the young man said. 'What do I still lack?'

Jesus answered, 'If you want to be perfect, go, sell your possessions and give to the poor, and you will have treasure in heaven. Then come, follow me.'

When the young man heard this, he went away sad, because he had great wealth.

Then Jesus said to his disciples, 'Truly I tell you, it is hard for someone who is rich to enter the kingdom of heaven. Again I tell you, it is easier for a camel to go through the eye of a needle than for someone who is rich to enter the kingdom of God.'

When the disciples heard this, they were greatly astonished and asked, 'Who then can be saved?'

Jesus looked at them and said, 'With man this is impossible, but with God all things are possible.'

On paper this guy's got it all – he's powerful (Luke 18:18 tells us he's a ruler), young and, as verse 22 tells us, loaded. He'd be all over the celeb magazines today. But there's something missing – he knows it himself; see what he's worried about in verse 16. Eternal life. Yes, he's got it all, but that's not enough.

What will happen when he dies? He's worried about eternity. And that's good, isn't it?

Well, yes, but sadly, he's not worried enough. There's lots we could say about this encounter – the way he recognises that Jesus has the answers, his mistaken belief that he must do some 'good thing' to get into heaven – but the key thing here is his failure to enter the kingdom of God.

First, isn't it ironic that this guy is called a ruler, but in reality he is being ruled by his money? It looks as if he has it all, but really his money and possessions have him. He could not bear to be parted from them. Jesus knew that they had become his god, his idol, and that they were standing between him and heaven.

YES, HE'S GOT IT ALL, BUT THAT'S NOT ENOUGH.

People have remarked that it's interesting that Jesus only quotes the second half of the Ten Commandments to this guy, the unspoken accusation being that he has failed in the first two – God is not number one in his life, and money has become his idol.

Even though this guy goes away sad, he still isn't willing to say goodbye to his wealth.

Jesus said to his disciples, 'Truly I tell you, it is hard for someone who is rich to enter the kingdom of heaven. Again I tell you, it is easier for a camel to go through the eye of a needle than for someone who is rich to enter the kingdom of God.' (vv. 23,24)

Jesus isn't saying we all have to give away everything to the poor like some kind of medieval hermit might have done, but if we could never cope without our money and possessions that is a huge warning sign that we are being ruled by the idol of money.

You probably don't have huge wads of cash at the moment, but maybe you're dreaming of the day when you'll get that student loan cheque and what you will spend it on. Maybe you enter those radio competitions dreaming of winning the big cash prize. Maybe your family has plenty of money and you just take a certain standard of living, with foreign holidays and all the latest electronic gadgets, for granted. But ultimately, money and 'things' can't give you lasting fulfilment.

RULED BY MONEY?

If money has already got its claws into you, then it's time for a counter-attack. How is it ruling us? Find the weak spot! First, it can tap into our fears. Do you worry about not having money? Do you rely on your mum or dad being able to dig you out of a hole if things get tight financially? Then you are looking to the idol of money for security.

Think of those bankers who committed suicide after the financial crash in 2009. They were not in charge of their money, it was in control of them, and they couldn't cope without it. They obviously felt unsafe and terrified at the thought of coping without it.

How else can money rule us? Well, spending it (and so getting hold of it) can become addictive. Do you ever catch yourself spending hours online – eBay or ASOS – deciding on your latest purchase? Is shopping one of your hobbies? The idol of money can make us feel good. Having money to spend gives us a buzz; it makes us feel better when we're low, or dynamic and powerful when we're up. If you've ever read the Confessions of a Shopaholic series or seen the film, you can see how easy it is to become addicted to spending.

THE IDOL OF MONEY CAN MAKE US FEEL GOOD.

Worshipping money can suck us into depending on it for security, and then looking to it for comfort or meaning and value. Don't forget Jesus' words of warning in Mark 8:36 – to paraphrase: 'What good is it for a girl to gain the latest Marc Jacobs handbag, but lose her soul? What good is it for a guy to be paid a Premier League salary, but lose his soul?'

However much you struggle with it now – and for most of us it's not having money rather than having it – the love of money will become far more of a danger to you when you leave home and start earning it for yourself. Resolve now to make money your servant and not your master.

USE IT OR LOSE IT

Don't forget that Jesus was far richer than we could ever be, and yet gave it all up for us:

> *For you know the grace of our Lord Jesus Christ, that though he was rich, yet for your sake he became poor, so that you through his poverty might become rich. (2 Cor. 8:9)*

Jesus offers the rich young ruler treasure in heaven in verse 21 of Matthew 19. It's an inheritance that Jesus' death has won for us. This is the only real sort of treasure. It is secure and lasting, as Jesus has already pointed out earlier in Matthew's Gospel:

But store up for yourselves treasures in heaven,
where moths and vermin do not destroy, and
where thieves do not break in and steal.
(Matt. 6:20)

And in the parable of the shrewd manager, Jesus makes the point that we can use our earthly wealth now to invest in eternity. Take a look at Luke 16:1–9.

Think what you can do with your money – fund gospel workers, support foreign missions, give to the poor and suffering. Money can be used as a tremendous force for good when you use it rather than worship it.

So use the money you have to store up everlasting treasure. Wouldn't it be great to meet people in heaven who wouldn't have heard the good news about Jesus unless someone told them – someone who was paid for by people like you?

YOU CANNOT SERVE GOD AND MONEY.

You cannot serve God and money. So serve God. That will probably not mean giving everything you have to the poor, but it will definitely involve going without stuff for the gospel. Remember Jesus' words that we started with in Mark 8?

'Whoever wants to be my disciple must deny

themselves and take up their cross and follow
me. For whoever wants to save their life will lose
it, but whoever loses their life for me and for the
gospel will save it. What good is it for someone to
gain the whole world, yet forfeit their soul?
Or what can anyone give in exchange for their
soul? (vv. 34–37)

Keep your eyes on what is *really* valuable. A famous missionary martyr, Jim Elliot, famously said: 'He is no fool who gives what he cannot keep to gain that which he cannot lose.'

There is a joke about a rich man who made a special deal with God to take a huge case full of gold ingots with him when he died. He arrived at the pearly gates and St Peter stopped him. 'I'm afraid you can't bring that in with you, sir,' he said.

'Oh yes I can,' said the rich man. 'I've made special arrangements.'

St Peter went away to check, and came back saying it had been given the OK. 'Do you mind if I take a quick look inside?' he asked.

'Be my guest,' said the rich man.

Opening the case, St Peter looked puzzled. 'Paving slabs?'

We are headed for a city paved with gold and built with jewels. Our heavenly inheritance in Christ far surpasses all this world has to offer. Don't get me wrong – tropical holidays, designer clothes and sports cars are amazing, but don't be seduced into worshipping wealth that will not last. All these things are just shadows of the riches that await God's people in the new creation. Going without now doesn't mean you're missing out. Ephesians chapter 1 talks about God blessing us with *every* spiritual blessing in Jesus and *lavishing* the riches of His grace (that is, His free, unearned favour) upon us (see vv. 3,7,8). God is not Scrooge, and neither should we be.

THINK IT OVER

- How does having/not having money make you feel?
- Read Philippians 4:11–13. Is that something you could say? Is it something you could pray for?
- How can you use money rather than let it rule you?
- Read Ephesians 1:3–14. What have we got if we belong to Jesus? How much better and more secure is that than top holidays, expensive gadgets and loads of cash?

CHAPTER 6:

TRY-DOL

In the movie *The Jungle Book* the ape King Louie tells Mowgli the mancub that he wants to be like him – he wants to walk into town, talk like a man, and have the power of making fire. He's not satisfied with being the jungle's VIP; he wants to fit in with people who he sees as superior to him (and I bet you're humming the song now!).

Haven't we all done that at some point? Bust a gut to look right, act right, and say the right thing to fit the image we are trying to present to the world? But what is the idol we risk worshipping here? Is it our appearance? Our sporting skills? Our fashion credentials? Our good behaviour? Our academic record? No, it goes deeper than that. When we put all our effort into maintaining an image, the idol we are worshipping is other people's approval.

Remember the definition of an idol? Something or someone we put in the place of God. And in this case it's the opinion of other people. When we are so bothered about looking a certain way, behaving a certain way or achieving certain things that it consumes our every waking moment, then other people's opinion of us has trumped God's. The approval of others has become the idol we are seeking so desperately to appease.

It's a very common idol and people were worshipping it way back in Jesus' day. Perhaps the worst offenders were the Pharisees – the religious leaders. See what Jesus has to say in Matthew 23:

Then Jesus said to the crowds and to his disciples: 'The teachers of the law and the Pharisees sit in Moses' seat. So you must be careful to do everything they tell you. But do not do what they do, for they do not practise what they preach. They tie up heavy, cumbersome loads and put them on other people's shoulders, but they themselves are not willing to lift a finger to move them.

'Everything they do is done for people to see: they make their phylacteries wide and the tassels on their garments long; they love the place of honour at banquets and the most important seats in the synagogues; they love to be greeted with respect in the market-places and to be called "Rabbi" by others. . . .' (vv. 1–7)

The Pharisees often get a bad press, but Jesus really lays into them here. Why? Well, one of the reasons can be seen in the verses above. Everything they do is to be seen by other people. They are not being 'religious' out of any genuine desire to worship God; nope, their idol is the approval and praise of other people. They are seeking to please human beings, not God.

There's something of that in us, isn't there? Be honest. We love to be approved of by others. When we wear the right things and fit in, when we look a certain way and get compliments, have the right hair, the right trainers, then we'll fit in, then people will like us, then we'll be happy. Our highest goal is for others to be pleased with us.

WE LOVE TO BE APPROVED OF BY OTHERS.

And it's not just about appearances, either. Our image is so much more than that. It's being 'the good girl', the sporty one, the funny one, the straight 'A' student. It's having a great profile picture, huge numbers of friends and constant witty status updates on Facebook.

There's a random philosophical question that goes something like this: 'If a tree falls in a forest and no one is around to hear it, does it make a sound?' Well, your guess is as good as mine on that one. But we might say, 'If I share a really funny FB status update and nobody "likes" it or comments, do I exist?'[1]

EVERYTHING WE DO IS DONE FOR PEOPLE TO SEE

There's a big problem with this idol. However hard we work to maintain the image, to please the idol of people's approval, we can't be the image we so desperately want to project.

In Emma Scrivener's brilliant book, *A New Name*, she writes about the different ways she tried and failed to fit in and to gain control of her life, eventually leading to anorexia:

I began by adopting a fresh persona – as class joker. While previously I had played it safe and blended in, now I became loud and reckless instead. My waking hours were spent inventing quips and planning new ways to entertain, always at my own expense. I affected a detachment to opinion and regaled my classmates with tall stories. Internally, however, I was in an agony of vigilance, measuring every word for its effect. I no longer knew who I was. All that mattered were the reflections mirrored back at me by my peers. Despite their laughter, I felt that they secretly despised me. How could they not? I slipped on bravado like my uniform, then left it bundled in a heap on the floor. Perhaps some traces of the old me remained, but she was unspeakably, obscenely ugly. I wanted her dead [2]

The problem with trying to maintain an image is that it is exactly that; an image, not reality. We have to straighten our hair, do more push-ups, hide the spots with make-up, pose for the photo and delete all the unflattering ones, work and slog to keep those good marks, come up with yet another funny remark, squashing and forcing ourselves into a particular mould to fit what we think other people will like.

IMAGE IS AN UNFORGIVING IDOL, A HARSH MASTER.

Image is an unforgiving idol, a harsh master. It is never satisfied, and seeking to serve it can enslave you just as much as its brother – money. So how do we free ourselves from it?

We are not good girls, sports stars or perfect students. We are grotty sinners, desperately looking for approval in all the wrong places. Emma worried that she was 'unspeakably, obscenely ugly', but the truth is, we all are.

See what Jesus says to the Pharisees:

'Woe to you, teachers of the law and Pharisees, you hypocrites! You clean the outside of the cup and dish, but inside they are full of greed and self-indulgence. Blind Pharisee! First clean the inside of the cup and dish, and then the outside also will be clean.

'Woe to you, teachers of the law and Pharisees, you hypocrites! You are like whitewashed tombs, which look beautiful on the outside but on the inside are full of the bones of the dead and everything unclean. In the same way, on the outside you appear to people as righteous but on the inside you are full of hypocrisy and wickedness. (vv. 25–28)

SKELETONS IN THE CLOSET?

But what good does it do us to gain the world's approval if we forfeit our souls? We might look good on the outside, but even if we fool some of the people some of the time, we can't fool God. Without Jesus, we are like a decaying corpse inside. Nice.

Only God can make us clean inside. Only Jesus can deal with our hypocrisy and wickedness. Ultimately, it's only His verdict which matters. If you were doing a test lap on *Top Gear*, you'd be listening to The Stig's feedback on your driving, not your mate who failed his test three times. Or imagine you baked a cake. If you wanted to know if it was any good, who would you ask? Your mum or Mary Berry? Well, your mum might be a great cake baker, but she's not going to be impartial, and unless she *is* Mary Berry then you'd probably still say Mary Berry's opinion would have more weight behind it. So, whose opinion counts? People at school, people in the street? Your family, your friends? Or God? We can't pretend that we're not affected by the opinion of people we care about. But step back for a minute and remember that God is the one who a) made us, b) died to save us and c) is making us into the people we were created to be. We have to admit that His opinion is the one that really counts.

ONLY GOD CAN MAKE US CLEAN INSIDE.

PLEASING GOD

So how do we please God? Jesus' disciples asked Him the very same question:

> Then they asked him, 'What must we do to do the works God requires?'
>
> Jesus answered, 'The work of God is this: to believe in the one he has sent.'
>
> (John 6:28,29)

Simple. Believe in Jesus. He offers us rest from the burden of people-pleasing, total acceptance and forgiveness for every single sin we have ever thought, said or done.

So what does God think of us? Remember, He sees our rotten hearts, the unclean bits that we are so good at covering up . . . We can never lie or pretend to God. He knows what we are like inside and out.

But get this. If you are believing in Jesus, when God looks at you He sees the life and track record of His perfect Son. He looks at us and says, 'You are my child, whom I love; with you I am well pleased' (see Mark 1:11).[3]

Seem impossible? Too good to be true? Well that's the awesome good news of the gospel! That's what will free us from serving the idol of self-image. We don't have to be good, sporty, clever, funny, successful and/or beautiful. We are loved, so we don't have to 'be' anything other than ourselves.

HIS VIEW OF YOU COULDN'T BE HIGHER.

When I was a student, I knew a wonderful elderly Christian lady. She was housebound and constantly worried that she was a burden to her family. She couldn't do anything for them, but they did everything for her. Do you think they saw it that way? No. They loved her and wanted to care for her, she didn't have to *do* anything to earn that love.

Don't strive and struggle to please the idol of other people's approval. You already have the unconditional acceptance and approval of the only One who counts. And His view of you couldn't be higher.

THINK IT OVER

- Whose approval really matters to you? Friends, family? And whose doesn't? Why?

- In what ways do you seek the approval of other people?

- If someone criticises you, how does it make you feel?

- What does God think about you?

Notes

1. Check out Tim Chester's *Will You Be My Facebook Friend?* (Chorley: 10Publishing, 2013) to think more about FB as a Christian.

2. Emma Scrivener, *A New Name* (Nottingham: IVP, 2012), p. 47.

3. Tim Keller's brilliant mini-book *The Freedom of Self-Forgetfulness* (Chorley: 10Publishing, 2012) is well worth a read on this topic.

CHAPTER 7:

THE END OF IDOLS

There's a moment in the film *Parental Guidance* when a girl who has been brought up by her slightly control-freak, healthy-lifestyle parents is given ice cream for the first time by her irresponsible grandparents. As she realises her parents have been conning her, she yells accusingly to her mum that ice cream tastes *nothing* like frozen yoghurt!

'Accept no substitutes', as the advertising slogan goes. The reality is always better than a poor imitation. We've seen that worshipping idols only occurs when God is pushed, squeezed or slips out of the centre of our lives. And equally the best way to displace and smash these idols is to replace them in our hearts and minds with the true and living God. Jesus is not only better then idols; He is *the best*, full stop!

Then he called the crowd to him along with his disciples and said: 'Whoever wants to be my disciple must deny themselves and take up their cross and follow me. For whoever wants to save their life will lose it, but whoever loses their life for me and for the gospel will save it. What good is it for someone to gain the whole world, yet forfeit their soul? Or what can anyone give in exchange for their soul? If anyone is ashamed of me and my words in this adulterous and sinful generation, the Son of Man will be ashamed of them when he comes in his Father's glory with the holy angels.' (Mark 8:34–38)

One day there will be no more idols. We will not be tempted to replace God with an inferior person or object. Why? Because one day we will see God face to face. As the apostle Paul puts it:

For now we see only a reflection as in a mirror; then we shall see face to face. Now I know in part; then I shall know fully, even as I am fully known. (1 Cor. 13:12)

We are heading for the end of this world when Jesus will come in His Father's glory with the holy angels. On that day, we will see dazzlingly clearly how empty and worthless our idols are. But for those who have held on to Jesus as the Christ – God's King – who have fixed their eyes and hearts on Him, there is a wonderful future. Check this out:

> Then I saw 'a new heaven and a new earth,' for the first heaven and the first earth had passed away, and there was no longer any sea. I saw the Holy City, the new Jerusalem, coming down out of heaven from God, prepared as a bride beautifully dressed for her husband. And I heard a loud voice from the throne saying, 'Look! God's dwelling-place is now among the people, and he will dwell with them. They will be his people, and God himself will be with them and be their God. "He will wipe every tear from their eyes. There will be no more death" or mourning or crying or pain, for the old order of things has passed away.' . . .

> I did not see a temple in the city, because the Lord God Almighty and the Lamb are its temple. The city does not need the sun or the moon to shine on it, for the glory of God gives it light, and the Lamb is its lamp. The nations will walk by its light, and the kings of the earth will bring their splendour into it. On no day will its gates ever be shut, for there will be no night there. The glory and honour of the nations will be brought into it. Nothing impure will ever enter it, nor will anyone who does what is shameful or deceitful, but only

those whose names are written in the Lamb's
book of life. (Rev. 21:1–4; 22–27)

We've seen that our idols cannot rescue us. They are just as much of a joke and an insult as the Israelites' golden calf back in Exodus. But Jesus can! See how He is described in the passage above – the Lamb. Back in the Old Testament, God's people had to sacrifice sheep and goats to pay for their sin over and over again, but Jesus died as a perfect sacrifice once and for all to bring us back to God (see 1 Pet. 3:18). We are no longer slaves to sin and headed for death without God. Jesus came to set us free.

WE'VE SEEN THAT OUR IDOLS CANNOT RESCUE US.

The anarchy we saw in Judges (and our own hearts) where there is no king is blasted out of the water here. God is on His throne (Rev. 22:1) and there will no longer be any curse (Rev. 22:3); we will be healed of our sin and our hurts forever (Rev. 21:4; 22:2).

Then the angel showed me the river of the water
of life, as clear as crystal, flowing from the throne
of God and of the Lamb down the middle of the
great street of the city. On each side of the river
stood the tree of life, bearing twelve crops of fruit,
yielding its fruit every month. And the leaves of

the tree are for the healing of the nations. No longer will there be any curse. The throne of God and of the Lamb will be in the city, and his servants will serve him. They will see his face, and his name will be on their foreheads. There will be no more night. They will not need the light of a lamp or the light of the sun, for the Lord God will give them light. And they will reign for ever and ever. (Rev. 22:1–5)

Ecclesiastes showed us the danger of seeking meaning and purpose in the idols of pleasure, success and possessions. Look at what we are destined for in Revelation 22:4,5 – being honoured with God's own mighty name and ruling the world in that name. And what about our hearts? We saw in Ezekiel how easily we give them to idols, but here we are witness to the ultimate love-match. Back in Ezekiel, the Temple was polluted by rubbishy idols, but now God's people have direct access and a perfect relationship with Him (Rev. 21:22). Revelation 21:2 shows God's people in God's new city as a radiant bride married to her loving husband, the Lord Jesus, for all eternity.

THE LORD GOD WILL GIVE THEM LIGHT.

But God is also our undisputed King. You cannot serve God and money as Matthew 6:24 reminded us, but one day we will gladly and wholeheartedly serve God (Rev. 22:3) in His rich and glorious city (see Rev. 21:9–27).

We will not have to please the idol of other people's approval; there is no place any more for desperately trying to impress others. Our future doesn't rely on anything we have done, but on our names being found in the Lamb's book of life (21:27). It's all down to what Jesus did on the cross. Because of His death and resurrection you are perfect, without spot or blemish (Eph. 5:27; Col. 1:22). It's God's opinion that matters, and He says we are His people and He will live with us forever (21:3).

In the C.S. Lewis book *The Last Battle*, a large number of people and animals are fooled into worshipping a donkey dressed up in a lion skin instead of the real Lion, Aslan. They only see the fake Aslan in near darkness and nobody is allowed to get too close in case they realise he is a poor imitation. When the real Aslan returns, the contrast is obvious.

Idols promise the world but fail to deliver. Jesus delivers. He is the real thing beside which the fake gods of self, sex, success, stuff and security suddenly look pathetic.

Jesus went to the cross for us. He suffered rejection by humanity and God, and tasted judgement and death so that we don't have to (Mark 8:31). But He rose again after three days, He guarantees our future and, if we follow Him, our lives will be eternally secure. One day He will return in His Father's glory with the holy angels. The sun will come up and the candle will be outshone.

THINK IT OVER

- Why will focusing on the future help us see through idols now?

- In what ways does Jesus blow your idols out of the water?

- What do you need to remember? Is there a Bible verse you could learn to help you?

- Spend some time talking to God now. Ask for the help of His Holy Spirit to turn away from your idols and ask Him to fill your heart with love for His Son.

a division of **10** of those.com

10Publishing is the publishing house of **10ofThose**.
It is committed to producing quality Christian
resources that are biblical and accessible.

www.10ofthose.com is our online retail arm selling
thousands of quality books at discounted prices.

For information contact: **sales@10ofthose.com**
or check out our website: **www.10ofthose.com**